# WHAT DOES A
# DEFENDER
# DO?

Paul Challen

**PowerKiDS**
press™

New York

Published in 2018 by The Rosen Publishing Group, Inc.
29 East 21st Street, New York, NY 10010

Developed and Produced for Rosen by BlueApple*Works* Inc.
Managing Editor for BlueApple*Works*: Melissa McClellan
Art Director: Tibor Choleva
Designer: Joshua Avramson
Photo Research: Jane Reid
Editor: Marcia Abramson

Photo Credits: Cover bikeriderlondon/Shutterstock; title page, p. 12 Stef22/Dreamstime.com; TOC Natursports/Shutterstock; TOC background, backgrounds p. 10, 14, 16, 26, 30, 32 romakoma/Shutterstock; page numbers EFKS/Shutterstock; backgrounds top p. 4, 8, 10, 14, 16. 20, 22, 26 Christian Bertrand/Shutterstock; backgrounds p. 6, 7, 13, 19, 24, 25, 28, 29 odd-add/Shutterstock; p. 4, 5, 8, 18 TJ Choleva; p. 6, 15 Louis Horch/Dreamstime.com; p. 7 James Boardman/Dreamstime.com; p. 9, 11, 29 muzsy/Shutterstock; p. 10 Matthew Trommer/Dreamstime.com; p. 13 Herbert Kratky/Shutterstock; p. 14 lev radin/Shutterstock; p. 16, 21, 27 right Natursports/ Dreamstime.com; p. 17 katatonia82/Shutterstock; p. 19 Keeton Gale/Shutterstock; p. 20, 21 top, 24 mooinblack/Shutterstock; p. 22 Paolo Bona/Shutterstock; p. 23 Steindy/ Creative Commons Attribution-Share Alike 2.0 Germany; p. 25 Monkey Business Images/ Shutterstock; p. 26 left Kostas Koutsaftikis/Shutterstock; p. 26 right AGIF/Shutterstock; p. 27 left Aspen Photo/Shutterstock; p. 27 top MaxiSports/Dreamstime.com; p. 28 katatonia82/Shutterstock; p. 30; back cover Krivosheev Vitaly

Cataloging-in-Publication Data
Names: Challen, Paul.
Title: What does a defender do? / Paul Challen.
Description: New York : PowerKids Press, 2018. | Series: Soccer smarts | Includes index.
Identifiers: ISBN 9781508154488 (pbk.) | ISBN 9781508154440 (library bound) |
   ISBN 9781508154365 (6 pack)
Subjects: LCSH: Soccer--Defense--Juvenile literature. | Soccer--Juvenile literature.
Classification: LCC GV943.9.D43 C53 2018 | DDC 796.334'2--dc23

Manufactured in China
CPSIA Compliance Information: Batch #BS17PK For Further Information contact: Rosen Publishing, New York, New York at 1-800-237-9932

# CONTENTS

# THE SOCCER TEAM

Eleven players make up a soccer team. Two teams play a game of soccer. Each team has a goalkeeper, the one player who remains in the goal and tries to keep the other team from scoring. The rest of the soccer team's players can move all over the field. Defenders, midfielders, and forwards — the remaining 10 **outfield players** — can play in many different formations.

*A soccer team's formation is described using numbers. Beginning with the number of defenders, then midfielders, and then forwards, this quick numbering system tells fans how a team will set up. A common 4-3-3 formation means that, along with the goalkeeper, a team will play with four defenders, three midfielders, and three attacking forwards.*

Winger
(Forward)

Center
Forward

Outside
Midfielder

Winger
(Forward)

Center
Midfielder

Outside Back
(Defender)

Outside
Midfielder

Center Back
(Defender)

Center Back
(Defender)

Goalkeeper

Outside Back
(Defender)

4-3-3 Formation

# THE ROLE OF THE DEFENDER

It's easy to guess what a defender's main job is from the name of their position – to protect their own goal and the area of the field closest to it. Defenders work together to stop opposing forwards, intercept passes, and block shots. They also play an important role in passing the ball to their teammates once they have won it from the other team. Defenders look to score when they have a chance, especially when they push up the field on **set pieces** like corner kicks and free kicks.

*The soccer field is also called the "pitch." The pitch has two goals on either side. Each goal has a 6-yard box, a penalty spot, and an 18-yard box in front of it. The end lines run behind each goal, and sidelines run along the sides. The center circle is right in the middle of the field. Corner flags and markings are in each of the four corners.*

Corner Flag

Goal

Corner Flag

Center Circle

Penalty Spot

Goal

18-yard Box

Sideline

6-yard Box

End Line

Soccer Field

# THE DEFENSIVE UNIT

Although soccer fans love to see their team score goals, it is impossible to win games without a strong defense. After all, it's great if a team can score four goals in a game — but they cannot win if their opponents score five or more goals!

All kinds of players can be successful on defense, but all defenders need to keep in mind that their primary job is to defend their goal by stopping opposing dribblers, cutting out passes, and blocking shots. Often, it is just as important to slow down an opponent as it is to win or intercept the ball.

*Some coaches believe in "building a team from the back." This means they will look for strong defensive players before they look for players who can score.*

Defenders who play in the middle of the field are called **center backs**. Those who defend on the wings are called **fullbacks** or outside backs. Both kinds of defenders combine as a defensive unit, moving up and down the field to prevent the opposing teams from having chances to score. It is very important for this unit to work together and for defenders to communicate with one another.

*Coaches looking to build strong teams, especially at a youth level, will often begin by putting the strongest players on defense. These coaches believe that preventing the opposing team from scoring should be their team's first priority.*

# DEFENSIVE STRATEGY

Any team that works to build a solid defense is actually also planning for a strong attack. This may seem odd, but in reality, being able to stop the opposing team from scoring can lead to quick counterattacks after the defense blocks a shot. When a team has a sound defense, attacking players know that they can push forward without the risk of the team being scored on easily.

How a team sets up its strategy often determines who wins the game.

From the 1960s to the 1980s, Italian teams achieved great success with a tight defensive style called "catenaccio," which translates to "door bolt." In catenaccio, defenders stay deep in their own half to lock the door to the goal. Catenaccio was widely used for a time, but most teams now seek more balance between offense and defense. Some teams do still use a catenaccio style of play — especially in Italy.

## DEFENDING SETUPS

A team can have as many defenders as the coach wants. A common setup is to play with four defenders — with two center backs in the middle and a fullback on either side. It is also common to use three or even five defenders. Coaches must always be aware that adding defenders means there will be fewer players available to play midfield and forward positions. A team can never have more than 10 outfield players at any one time, so it's important to balance defense and offense.

*Before each match, coaches tell players what to expect from the opponent and what strategy and formation to use.*

9

# DEFENSIVE SKILLS

To be a defender in soccer, you need good balance, physical strength, and speed. All of these are important to be able to stop opposing attackers. Defenders also need good foot skills for making long and short passes, dribbling, and even shooting.

Of all the players on a team, defenders must have the greatest jumping ability to head balls in the air. They also must be able to lunge powerfully in all directions to make strong tackles. Defenders must be able to "read" how a game is developing in front of them.

*It is important for defenders to communicate well, especially center backs who are constantly giving instructions to their teammates from the middle of the pitch.*

# COVERING THE GROUND

Soccer experts often speak about "keeping shape" on defense. That means that a team's defenders must avoid gaps opening up between one another. Keeping a good **defensive shape** makes it hard for opposing attackers to pass the ball to teammates or to dribble and shoot on goal. To maintain shape, defenders must communicate with one another, watch each other's positioning on the pitch, and keep track of opposing attackers.

*After winning the ball, it is crucial for a defender to make accurate passes to teammates, rather than simply kicking the ball away. All of the effort involved in winning a ball is wasted if the defender gives the ball to the opposing team with a careless pass!*

# CENTER BACKS

Because of the work they do in the middle of the pitch, central defenders are at the heart of every team's defense. Strong center backs allow a team to successfully stop opposing attackers, and give their teammates the confidence to push forward and attack. Center backs can also play an important role in free kicks and corner kicks. They are often outstanding at heading the ball, and sometimes even score!

*Strong center backs put everything on the line for their team. Such fearless play earns them respect, so they often become team captains.*

It is common for a team to play with two center backs. This partnership means that both players work as a pair to protect the goal. Good center back pairs cover one another so that if one steps forward to tackle or intercept a pass, the other drops back to protect the space behind. It is also crucial for center backs to communicate with their goalkeeper at all times.

The most important skill a center back needs is tackling. Center backs must win the ball cleanly and fairly, but must also aggressively challenge opposing attackers. Because they often play so close to their own goal, center backs must be careful not to give away penalties by fouling opponents in their own penalty areas.

*Center backs must be experts in using strength and body positioning to keep opponents away from the ball.*

# STOPPERS AND SWEEPERS

Some teams use two center backs in what is known as a **stopper/sweeper setup**. This means that one center back plays in front of the other. The center back closer to the midfielders is the stopper. This player's role is to stop any attacks as they develop in the defensive third of the pitch.

The sweeper, who is also known as the last line of defense, plays behind the stopper. This player's job is to sweep up any offensive passes that get past the stopper and the other defenders.

*Teams that use the stopper/sweeper setup are very concerned with defense and often play with the main goal of stopping the other team from scoring, rather than scoring themselves.*

Both stoppers and sweepers need speed, agility, and strong ball-winning skills. They must be outstanding communicators, and they need to be very alert so that they know what is going on around them at all times. Although they must be aggressive when defending, they must also have the finesse to make accurate passes when in possession of the ball, and a wide range of heading, dribbling, and shooting skills as well.

# FULLBACKS

Fullbacks are the defenders who take up positions on the outside of the defensive line. Because of this, many soccer fans in the United States call these players outside backs. Given their wide positions, one of the main jobs of fullbacks is to cover the fast attacking wingers of the opposing team.

Fullbacks must understand how to position themselves in cooperation with center backs and midfielders so they are not stranded on the outside of the field and not taking part in defensive play.

Fullbacks are often smaller and speedier than center backs. Because they play farther away from their own goal, they are more likely to be skillful dribblers.

## FULLBACK SKILLS

Fullbacks must be strong runners. They need speed to keep up with opposing attackers, and good endurance to run up and down the wings all game. As defenders, they must be good at tackling and winning the ball. Fullbacks need a range of short and long passing techniques. When they get forward into the opposing half of the field, they must be able to deliver accurate **crosses**. Although they must be good at headers, their ability to head balls is not as important as it is for center backs.

*Because of their position to the side and back of a team, fullbacks are often called on to take throw-ins for their team when the ball goes out of bounds.*

# THE WINGBACK

The **wingback** is a relatively new position in soccer. Wingbacks are a combination of fullbacks and attacking wingers, and cover a lot of space up and down the outside of the pitch.

A wingback's job is a combination of stopping opposing wingers and pushing up the wings with the ball to cross the ball. Because of this, wingbacks must be tireless, fast runners with the ability to cross accurately. They must always be on the alert for passes from their teammates as they move forward to attack.

*Coaches usually use wingbacks in a five-player defensive setup along with three center backs, or as part of a five-player midfield with three center midfielders.*

Forward

Forward

Center Midfielders

Wingback
(Defender)

Center Backs
(Defenders)

5-3-2 Formation

Wingback
(Defender)

Goalkeeper

# OVERLAPPING RUNS

Although a fullback's main job is to defend, many teams also use these players to make what are called **overlapping runs**. This is an important attacking move and can lead to goal-scoring chances for teams who use it well. On an overlapping run, a fullback will run without the ball to the outside of a midfield teammate. By running past and to the outside of the midfielders, the fullback gets in a good position to receive a pass. When the fullback receives the pass, they have the option to beat a defender and cut in towards goal or send a cross in from an outside position.

Even if the overlapping fullback does not get a pass after making the run, he or she will take along a defender to cover the run. This means there is more space to attack in the middle of the pitch.

# DEFENDERS IN ATTACK

Although defenders are vital in stopping opponents from scoring, many teams also use defenders as an important part of their attack. For example, central defenders can make runs with the ball out of defense, beat opponents with dribbles, and make passes to their teammates rushing towards the goal. It takes a lot of skill and the ability to read the game well for a center back to play this way, but when done correctly, it can be an important attacking weapon.

*Spanish speedster Jordi Alba is a great example of a defender who also stars on offense. He plays for Barcelona and for his national team.*

You don't have to be big to be a defender. In 2006, Fabio Cannavaro of Italy became the first defender to win FIFA World Player of the Year for his role on Italy's World Cup championship team. Cannavaro played as center back despite being only 5 foot 9 (175 cm). He made up for his lack of height with great jumping ability and determination.

Attacking defender plays are not just about one player, however. Teams that play this way must know how to cover the gaps left by center backs who leave their standard positions to attack. If the ball is lost when a central defender is going forward, somebody needs to be there to cover them on defense. Also, a team that uses fullbacks to attack down the wings (see page 19) must make sure that these attacks are covered by teammates.

It is common for defenders, and especially center backs, to leave their positions at the back when their team is taking a free kick or corner kick. These players are often the tallest players on teams, so they have a good chance of heading aerial balls towards the goal.

# OFFSIDE

Defenders must know the offside rule in soccer in great detail. This rule says that an attacking player cannot be behind the last defender (not including the goalkeeper) when a pass is played forward in their attacking half of the field. This prevents attacking players from cherry picking, or waiting behind the last defender for the ball to be kicked towards them in an attempt to rush in and score.

*Because the offside rule says that a player cannot be offside when the ball is kicked forward to them, there are many close calls involving this timing. It is the main responsibility of the assistant referee (often called the linesman) to call offsides.*

# THE OFFSIDE TRAP

To try to put opposing forwards offside, defenders will often push up past the attacker. This is an important defensive move called the offside trap. To execute the trap correctly, defenders must work as a unit to push forward to force opponents offside. If one defender lags back, they may keep the opposing player onside, so all defenders must be aware of each other's position to execute the trap. Also, the defenders must always be ready to chase back if this trap doesn't work. Finally, defenders must communicate with their goalkeeper who must sweep up if a ball gets through the trap.

*If a team successfully plays the offside trap, an attacker will be caught offside.*

# THE ROLE OF A HEAD COACH

The head coach of a professional soccer team is sometimes also known as the manager. Head coaches decide which players will start each game, and which substitutions will be used. They also decide what strategy a team will use, and what formation it will play.

Head coaches play an active role during games, yelling instructions to players from the sidelines. Professional teams have several assistant coaches who help the head coach in training and in games.

Along with their assistant coaches, head coaches help a team work on various aspects of the game of soccer through training. This can include individual ball skills, passing, defending, or team tactics. At the higher levels of the game, head coaches watch videos of opposing teams before games to notice their strengths and weaknesses. Head coaches and assistants also help players work on fitness and individual skills, both on the field and in the gym and weight rooms.

*Many defenders go on to become coaches when their playing days are over, bringing the leadership skills they have learned on the pitch to a teaching role.*

# THE BEST DEFENDERS

Top defenders include Italy's Paolo Maldini, who led AC Milan to an amazing 26 trophies in his 25 years with the club. He also captained the Italian national team for eight years. Another famous defender is German legend Franz Beckenbauer, who was known as "Der Kaiser" ("The Emperor") because of his dominant performances on defense. England's Bobby Moore captained the team that won the 1966 World Cup, and he is considered one of the all-time great defenders.

*Juventus defender Giorgio Chiellini (left) is also a top player for the Italian national team. Chiellini is known for his tough tackling and perfect positional sense.*

*Germany's Jerome Boateng (right) has excelled at both fullback and center back for Bayern Munich and his national team, winning the World Cup in 2014.*

Center back Laurent Koscielny stars for Arsenal in the English Premier League and the French national team. Germany's Phillip Lahm has an incredible mix of technical skill and soccer smarts. A fullback who can also play in central midfield, he captained his national team to the 2014 World Cup title. American Becky Sauerbrunn is an Olympic gold medalist and World Cup winner who has the distinction of having played every minute of every game for the United States in its 2015 World Cup win.

# BE A GOOD SPORT

Sportsmanship is at the heart of soccer, and it is one of the reasons the sport is also called "the beautiful game." Along with the official rules of the game, there are many unwritten rules that are unique to soccer. For example, even pro players often help an opponent who has fallen down up off the pitch. Teams do not run up a big score against a weaker team, and they kick the ball out of bounds when an opponent is injured so they can receive treatment.

*Even at the highest levels of soccer, such as the World Cup, fair play is considered very important by fans and players alike.*

# RESPECTING THE REFEREES

*Even though referees try to do the best job they can, they can make mistakes. Players, parents, and coaches need to respect the refs — no matter what the level of play. Yelling at the refs or loudly disputing calls is not good sportsmanship, and rarely helps a team. Also, it is important to keep in mind that in youth soccer, many referees are young people just learning how to referee.*

## RESPECT

A team receiving respectful treatment will also give that respect back to opponents. Even though it is important for soccer players to give 100 percent effort in games and training, trying to win should never be more important than showing respect for teammates and opponents. After all, everyone on the field and on the bench wants to have a fair game where everyone is treated well.

*Respect is also important for coaches, parents, and fans. Young players should remember that it never hurts to give a big thanks to the people who help and support them in developing their skills and building their love of the game.*

# GLOSSARY

**center backs** Central defensive players.

**crosses** Aerial passes, usually delivered from the wing with the intention of being headed on goal.

**defensive shape** The alignment of a team's defensive players.

**formation** The arrangement of the 10 outfield players on a soccer team.

**fullbacks** Outside defensive players.

**outfield players** All the players on a soccer team except those who are goalkeepers.

**overlapping runs** A tactic used by defenders (usually fullbacks or wingbacks) to run past and to the outside of a midfielder into an attacking position.

**set piece** A term used in soccer that refers to a situation when the ball is returned to open play, for example, following a stoppage in a game.

**stopper / sweeper setup** An arrangement of two center backs where one (stopper) takes up a more aggressive position and the other (sweeper) remains as the deepest defender.

**tackling** In soccer, the skill needed to win the ball legally from an opponent.

**wingback** An outside defensive position combining elements of fullback and midfield play.

# FOR MORE INFORMATION

## FURTHER READING

Doeden, Matt. *The World's Greatest Soccer Players*. Sports Illustrated, 2010.

Jökulsson, Illugi. *Stars of Women's Soccer*. Abbeville Kids, 2015.

Nixon, James. *Defending and Goaltending*. Smart Apple Media, 2012.

## WEBSITES

Due to the changing nature of Internet links, PowerKids Press has developed an online list of websites related to the subject of this book. This site is updated regularly. Please use this link to access the list:

**www.powerkidslinks.com/ss/defender**

# INDEX